Motherhood:
Journey
Into
Love

An Anthology of Poetry
from *Welcome Home*

Edited by
Edwina Peterson Cross

Illustrations selected by
Cathleen F. Gardner

Published by **Mothers At Home**®
Vienna, Virginia

Cover design by Cathleen F. Gardner
Marbleized paper on cover by Susan F. Douglas

© 1997 by Mothers At Home®, Inc.

Typesetting by Richman Hills Publications

Library of Congress Cataloging-in-Publication Data
Motherhood — journey into love :   an anthology of poetry from Welcome
   home   /   edited by Edwina Peterson Cross   ;   illustrations selected by
   Cathleen F. Gardner.
      p.   cm.
   ISBN 0-9631188-2-X
      1. American poetry — 20th century.   2. Mother and child — Poetry.
   3. Motherhood — Poetry.   4. Mothers — Poetry.   I. Cross, Edwina
   Peterson.   1953-   .   II. Welcome home.
   PS595.M64M693   1997
   811′ .540803520431 — DC21

                                                                    97-8268
                                                                      CIP

Table of Contents

Preface

A thought, a dream, a vision
Stitched separately, then woven as a whole
Our songs of love, loss, and learning
Grief, growth, and joy,
Lyric moments of delight and doubt, faith and fears,
Wonder, wisdom, hope

With words shared and strengthened
Our singing
Expands the heart and unlocks time
Bringing smiles, empathy,
memories, tears

Age-old epic
Sweet and new as tomorrow's breath
A thought, a dream, a vision
Created, collected
Complete

I am deeply grateful to the many people who helped to make this dream become a reality. First and foremost are the past and present staff and volunteers of the national nonprofit organization Mothers At Home. Their philosophy and conviction provided the foundation on which this collection was built. All the poems contained in this anthology came from the pages of *Welcome Home*, the monthly journal of Mothers At Home. Throughout their richness and diversity runs a strong thread of camaraderie, support and sense of community. This is what is offered each month by *Welcome Home* to mothers who have chosen to devote their time and talents to nurturing their families.

I wish to thank everyone at Mothers At Home who assisted with this collection from conception to publication. I am especially grateful to Cathy Myers and Laura Jones, whose dedication, hard work, expertise, and insights were invaluable. Special thanks go to Cathy Gardner for her thoughtful selection of the beautiful art that makes this book whole and for her diligent effort and grace under the pressure of deadlines while accomplishing the design and layout. I also appreciate the editorial assistance of Eileen Doughty, Marian Gormley, Betsy Kocsis, Nancy Vazquez, Maureen Wade, and Betty Walter.

I am grateful to my children Lezlie, April, and Taran for their patience, understanding, and acceptance. They are the light of my life and the inspiration for my work. Special appreciation goes to my husband Verlin whose continuing effort and support have made it possible for me to be at home with our children and have given me the time and space for my work with *Welcome Home*, this book, and my own growth as an artist. I dedicate my work on this book to my mother, Zetta Benson Peterson, who taught me about poetry, mothering, and love.

Finally, my gratitude and admiration go to the poets who have shared their dreams, their heartaches, and their wealth of beautifully wrought words. From our separate songs, together we have woven a symphony.

—*Edwina Peterson Cross*

Motherhood: Journey Into Love

Charcoal drawing by Erika Lauver

"Mother"

A word is spoken
and I become

A paradox
of giving and receiving
nurturing and waiting
holding tight and letting go

An eternal vessel
waiting to be filled
with unimaginable
unfathomable
love

A word is spoken
ancient
much used
but, *this* time it is
mine
and will become
my name
my future
my heartbeat
my life

A word is spoken
and the pathway of my life
is forever colored
by this prism
All experiences now refracted
through its light

Life stretches out before me
washed with rainbows
and I begin
my
journey
into love

Edwina Peterson Cross

Sonogram

"Live" from inside my womb
a tiny form swims
in a dollop of black that resembles
the fluid in lava lamps.

Self-absorbed, paddling through evolution,
we scientifically measure you with ultrasonic waves.

Did you hear a sonic boom in your private watery chamber
above the whoosh
of my blood traveling through
those interstate arteries?

On the screen
you made an entrance into my consciousness - -
a somersaulting snail-darter
a depth charge
in my heart

Beth L. Foote

First Movement

Fishtail flutter
butterfly kiss

Dandelion dewdrop
Pussywillow whisper

Hummingbird quiver
spider web shimmer

Honey,
I think the baby kicked.

Sue Stormoen

Ink drawing by Debi Cole

Lullabye

On the edge of motherhood
And the shelf of a swing
She dreams—
Her hands cupped in cradle
For her chin,
Her belly an odd round,
A bare silence pressing in
And out
In swing rhythms.

She,
More a mother
For her dreams,
Is gentle with imagining
And sings
In the breeze
To the tremble
Of child.

Beth Kephart Sulit

Ink drawing by Katie Caulk

Waiting For You

After the fourth night
 of a labor that began and quit
  I am truly a woman in waiting.
With painfully swollen feet
  and tender emotions
I soaked until the shower ran cold
 wondering about you.
You kicked and squirmed
 as I wondered,
not what you'll be someday,
 but who;
not how I'll feel when first I touch
 your newborn skin
  but how I'll ever, in all my life,
find a way of expressing it to you.
I wondered if,
 when you are old enough to care,
  you'll like your "coming home" clothes
  of rich violet and deep green
or if my image of you is too feminine
  or not feminine enough.
I wondered if I'll be courageous at your birth
  and if you'll ever give birth yourself.
I wondered if you'll come tonight
  or make me wait
yet another day
 to see you look wide-eyed at me
and let me fall in love
 at last
  with you.

Robin Rice Morris

Charcoal drawing by Erika Lauver

The Wait

My belly,
taut and smooth
A ball,
rolling and jerking
beneath a thin layer
Invisible
yet tangible to my touch

She will emerge,
slick and angry
howling at the invasion
of her solitude,
Changing mine
forever.

Soon, soon

These empty arms
will be full of the
unimaginable
My other self,
a mystery
finally revealed.

Soon, soon

This vigil will end
I wait to meet
my shadow
and yearn
for time to stop,
slow down, speed up,
to be now.

Joan R. Wollin

The Walk

I will take you for a walk
down the winding gravel road
to the lake. Afternoon sun bathes
the fields of alfalfa and standing corn
green and golden in the autumn light.
The wind is brisk
skipping brittle leaves across the stones
in my path. Maples bleed
on the edges, harbingers of summer's
end.

I will take you for a walk.
It is the least that I can do.
I can not give you more,
can not give you endless days of sun
or nights full of stars
just this brief afternoon under an
autumn sky.

I will be this day
the senses you will never know
the eyes that will not live
to see such a day.
I will drink in
the scent of tall grasses
the clover and vetch,
spy the blue cornflower faded against
the rail fence,
bend my eye across waving fields
to the far tumble of hills,
let the strong breeze rove through my
hair
myself alive and here.

I do this for you, while you are still
while we are still one
while tears flow down cheeks
that wanted so to hold you near and kiss
your own so flushed and lovely face

I am not the first woman who ever lost a
child.
But you are the first child I have ever
lost.
I do not know what else to do but walk.

Now the road curves, meets the water's
edge
a savannah of sparkling blue
stretches west framed by the black stone
beach
and distant hills. The mountains rise
behind
like sentinels guarding against the
passage
of this day. I sit,
a piece of driftwood at my feet.
Here the wind blows hard.
Though the water is low, waves are high
urged on by the driving breeze. A
seagull
circles, then drops to a rock outcrop in
the bay.

I share this with you. It is just
the two of us here now, one being the
eyes and breath and body for both.
I know that I will lose you soon.
And not being able to hold onto more
I hold to this day and you in my
memory
perfect as an afternoon blessed by wind
and sun
water moving under the sky
and summer's fire burned into autumn
leaves.

Katherine H. Maynard

Watercolor by Krista Skelton

Watercolor by Downey Dress

Shifting

I leave my computer monitor,
  air-conditioned Honda,
    the elevator
to lie sacrificially on this table.

No brilliant new age advancements
     prepared me
for this awkward spreading of my legs.

No technology alters the fact that someone's head
      is wedged
in a place unmentioned over lets-do-lunch.

Not labor.
Wrenching, sweeping
Overwhelming ripping,
pushing, pulling
  Hot white war

Two births, not one:
  Mother and Child.

Saddle sore
  Breast heavy,
I hold my son in aching arms.
  Stare in his eyes,
    Tickle his cheek with my own,
      And promise us both
I will be MOTHER.

I will be Lace White Apron, All Good Feeder
Tire Not Caresser, Book Reader, Rainbow Finder
Gentle Strong Maternal One.

Time passes
  and passes
    and passes.
Now maybe I am and maybe I'm not.
Maybe I am myth.
Maybe I am only necessity.
I cannot tell.
  Reality has been recast.

And Somehow,
     I'm still
       In labor.

Leanne Thompson Worwood

Inland Seas

I am a continent in the making,
my belly stretches and changes shape,
the skeleton shifting,
expanding,
emotions erupting,
sometimes quiet after the storm.

Inside you are an island,
the shape and contour of you
turning over and over.

Although the sea flowing around you
connects us,
and protects you as breezes blow overhead
through your island forests,
we are also separate,
my continent's upheaval continues,
your mass expanding.

One clear morning
I woke to a storm brewing clouds,
the heat mounting,
waves crashing the beaches of your tiny shores
until the root that held you tightly
in place broke loose, and you were thrown
into the current,
sometimes bumping along the coastline,
sometimes caught in the shallows,
in the eye of the storm,
sometimes in the storm itself,
as wind and water rushed at you from all sides.

One final push
and you are free,
drift into the river's mouth
as it empties into the ocean.

Now I cradle you, little island,
into contours of a shrinking continent,
in these first moments of life
quietly rocking you,
listening to your sighs float
up into a broader sky.

Heather Grant

Watercolor by Jan Myers

Birth Song

The old voice at my side
    Is not my husband; No
    He cannot know this pain
    Though he courageously tries.
    The language is not mine
    But her words encourage
    You Can! You Must! Again!
    My breathing keeping time.
    Each pain grows strong and long
    She sends me to my core
    Where strength glows like a beacon
    And kindles the birthing song.
    Her voice belongs to many
    Women from all cultures, times
    Linked hand-in-hand across the earth
    They rise to comfort me.
    My cry joins them as they sing
    In a hoarse, triumphant shout
    Bearing a gift into this world
    That only a woman can bring.

Tamara O. Perdue

Adopted Miracle

While I was grieving
  you were growing.
When my world was ripped apart
  yours was safe, sound, secure.
In my darkest hour of sorrow
  you knew another kind of darkness—
  a pre-birth warmth—
And while I mourned
  you found your way
    to the light
      and to me.

You were the sunshine
  breaking through my storm clouds.
You brought life
    joy
      love
  and I cannot give enough
  in return.
Your existence redefines mine
And I can only whisper
  as I watch your sleeping form
I love you
  my precious, precious
      daughter.

Donna-Jean A. Breckenridge

Ink drawing by Anne Baumgartner

18   Pencil drawing by Jeanne Derwin

Baby Milk

early winter morning
autumn baby,
you whimper, searching
for my milk

you find me
in the darkness
your lips speak silent words
upon my breast
and wait

I press you gently
against me
caress your tiny thigh
unleash a sigh
that lets my milk
unravel

like velvet ribbon
smooth and warm
it comforts us,
wrapping us
in sleepy bliss

Cheryl Racanelli

A Balm

we slept late today
then I lay awake
nose to nose with you
smelling your sweet breath
watching the rise and fall of your tiny
    shoulder

being a grown-up is hard sometimes
drinking in your baby sweetness
is a balm to my troubled soul.

Marcia Crosbie

19

When Neighbors Have Their Babies

The neighbors' truck roars into life
    at three a.m.,
    waking me on setting out to have their
    second born.
I shake my sleeping husband;
    "They're leaving for the hospital," I say.
He grunts and goes serenely back to sleep.
I lie beside him, restless,
    remembering past rendezvous with
    birthing rooms:
    the midnight pangs, clock-watching, the
    endless wait
    until the first cry, healthy,
    consummates the agonized uncertainty.
I get up then,
    pad noiselessly to visit children's rooms:
    the elder, slightly snoring,
    hugs the bear he now disdains by
    daylight;
    the younger, sweet and rosy,
    like a flower's heart is curled
    within the petals of her sheets.
Then I go back to bed and stare at darkness.
I know now that when neighbors have their
    babies,
    husbands sleep;
    their wives, awake, remember.

Victoria Everitt

Meditation in
a Rocking Chair

little buddha head on my shoulder
so warm so soft so heavy
mind wanders to past and future
things to do, projects unfinished
restless

or I can repose
in the soft stillness
of the moment
and your wide baby eyes

be here now
ever now
ever more deeply alive
to this quiet joyful present magic

Marcia Crosbie

Ink drawing by Lisa Beth Brown

Ink drawing by Pam Collar

The First Four Months
Are The Hardest

Wash, diaper, nurse.
Repeat.
Step over
fermenting piles
of soiled Onesies.
Rock the baby.
Sing to the baby.
Feed the baby at 2 a.m.
Feed the baby at 4 a.m.
Wake with the baby at 6 a.m.
Calling all parents—
unshowered, sleep-deprived,
nerves massaged by barbed wire.
Shuffle cribside
and behold the rested infant.

Renewal surges forth like a symphony
in a single gummy smile.

Margaret Ashburn Krajeski

Work-day Morning

As I came awake
the sun had not quite risen
Half asleep I check the cradle
only to find my son sleeping in his mother's arms

"Angelic" is not enough to describe the two
resting in the folds of their mutual softness.
Peace and love and warmth surround the pair
as they sleep

All I can do is quietly stare and wonder
how such exquisite beauty is possible

Then I reluctantly have to go
Leaving them to their rest
To do whatever I can
To allow this miracle to continue

Ed Peterson

To Other Mothers

When you tidy up after the day
Where do you put away
your fears?

That twist of worry
looping its way
around the love,
threads of dread entwined
with winding happiness.

At night
do you undo your heart,
brush out the long shining contentment,
yank at intractable tangles of worry,
dig your fingers into the knotted fear?

Then twist
the whole unruly bundle back together,
tying it tight with your bright
everyday ribbons?

Each night as she sleeps I lean again
over her bed,
these tears on my lips,
these words in my eyes—

Empty hands hoping
helpless heart trying
once more
to find the right prayer.

Seema V. Atalla

Sleep Tight

Evening slips into the room
and
I think about you . . .
As I tuck teddy bears
around my little son.

We'd sit and weave dreams
you and I
while the stars whispered
summer
through the Venetian blinds.

You'd tuck white percale
around me
and
I didn't want to say
"good night."
It was so final, mommie.

I think about you . . .
As I tuck teddy bears
around my little son.

Carola Van Heukelom

Watercolor by Joyce Elliott

My Sister's Child

I am not new at this—

I have two children of my own—
Yet, when I held you cradled in one
    arm,
your tiny fingers, clinging fast to me,
Unknowingly, you clutched
more than my dress;
My very heart fell right
within your grasp
as strange emotions took me by surprise
And I could see a sadness in your eyes
(or were those mine?)
Reflecting needs I do not
wish to face . . .
I'm growing older.
Soon I will not have the choice to make,
My body will retire from mothering,
my womb lay empty for eternity,
No tenant renting fertile space within
while gaining strength and
humanness from me
Like some small seedling
wrapped in flesh cocoon
soon sprung to beauteous
independent flight
While I stand proudly
watching you emerge . . .
But wait—you are not mine;
You are my sister's child.
Still, I will stay and
hold you for a while.

Valerie Rossetti

On Leavetaking

Goodbye is not my word.
Today I stand at the half-open
door and think: though the sky fall
in jagged pieces at my feet,
I will not go. My life
is here, my roots curl
into the earth,
and disappear.

Let others go who need
adventure. Mine is here
beneath a changeling sky, rooted
on this heedless earth tumbling
through time. Taking
not a single step I spin
through eons of eternity,
and sometimes catch my breath
on the point of a star: all
from this scarred doorstep.
What is far? Search deep
if you would know.

Wendy McVicker

6-13-89

All week I've wished you would
play more independently
so I could "get something done."

Now you are

and I can't

I sit fascinated
intent on your every move
and expression
enjoying

my heart caught in your net.

Marcia Crosbie

Getting It

To be content, I must create.
A work of art, of literature, of science;
Something unique, something my own.
And to be happy, truly happy,
My creation must be recognized,
Acclaimed, and enduring.

How sad, his wife replied,
That evoking a smile, teaching a lesson,
Watching a sunset, relieving a burden
Provide you with neither contentment
Nor happiness.

You don't get it, he shouted.
Thank goodness, she sighed.

Robert Deluty

Ink drawing by Jami Moffett

First Birthday

My baby, now toddling quickly
into your next dimension,
the long days we've shared together
have enchanted and delighted me,
sleep-deprived and overwhelmed me.
Each day unfolds a new you.
A year to discover you,
A lifetime to love you.
Moment by moment
day by day
precept upon precept
My second son, you've proved the timeless saga—
a mother's love stretched does not break the heart,
it only magnifies it.
My devotion to you is as fierce as a gale,
as soft as a whisper
and all the mundane in-betweens.
Does every mother feel that no one has ever loved
like her before?

Carol Mader

Watercolor by Kelly Gallaher

Phone Call To My Mother

Oh, marvelous magic
Mystical box
Powerful tiny enchanted thing
Cradled in my hand
My fingers brush its surface
Dancing out a secret code
Drumming out a private incantation
Drawing forth the magic
Delivering unseen glamours into the thin bright air
And suddenly . . .
From out of nothingness . . .
I conjure you
Invoke your voice from far away
Just by the tappings of my sapient secret spell
I have captured you in the palm of my hand!
And here I will spellbound hold you
and pour out upon you all the happenings of my day
Wrap you in the pages of each book I have read
Bathe you in the sparkles of my children's laughter
Into the tiny box around you I will pack all my loneliness
The sharp jagged pieces of my pain
And you will sing me all smooth again
Disembodied beloved voice
Summoned genie in a box
Marvelous magical mystery box
Powerful tiny enchanted thing
Cradled in my hand

Edwina Peterson Cross

Multiple Me

Are you kidding? I'm not
searching for identity.

Some plural definition maybe.
Why, there are pieces of me
emerging
all over the place,
talk about growth as a person—
I'd put a hydra to shame,
heads shooting from every fingertip.
Which person
do I grow as?

Nedda Davis

Pencil drawing by Deborah Simmons

33

Watercolor by Cathleen F. Gardner

Thanksgiving

full November moon
air strangely mild
your warm small hand in mine
we walk a winding wooded road
chattering with two-year-old questions.

"They're a lot of company"
croaked my neighbor once, fondly
a mountain lady
plump, toothless, blind.
She remembers.

I can almost see the gnomes and fairies
dancing in this dazzling silver light.

My heart swells, bursts
saturated with gratitude
with your sweetness
and the sharing of this with you.

Marcia Crosbie

Evening

As a woman wears her finest jewels
So I adorn myself with you
Draped around my neck and chest
    you lay
A beauty from my rough oyster body
Glowing pearly skin and eyes like
    gems
Wrestled from the dark Korean earth
I wear you proudly, sometimes
    vainly,
A passionate gift from my beloved.
Sleep still, my nighttime necklace,
    unawares,
Let me hold you longer 'til we
    outgrow
Such luxuries.

Kelly A. Kim

Baby Book

Nothing to talk about,
no photos to show
weight: a few ounces, height: unknown,
first word: not spoken.

The babies carve their initials into me;
even the children I almost had
but lost
claim a blue vein or a soft
round of skin for indelible entries.

Small, almost people, torn
and left behind in rooms of perfect light
antiseptic walls and impeccable behavior.

I recognize mothers of loss:
we sign the air in
supermarkets and doctors' offices
with runes that fade like smoke,
women whose arms, now filled by

lively children,
hold, somewhere else, another child we
almost knew, had named
secretly in our stunned silence.

Beth Joselow

Walking With My Friend
On Saturday Morning

We took our customary walk
along the creek beneath the trees
mosaic shadows in our path;
and as we talked I slipped the burden
off my shoulders
to see what chafed so painfully.

We peered inside, then
took the parts into the light
pondering each edge and angle.
I saw no censure in her eyes
no pleasure in my misery;
she carried much for me that day.

Later when we said good-bye
I gathered up my stock and stones,
put them on my back, and found
that turning them about and over
had smoothed the gnawing corners down
and eased the crushing load.

Linda H. Carney

Ink drawing by Sandra Littell

Pencil drawing by Marta Misleh

Two Hearts

Yesterday, I lay
and listened as a machine discovered
within me, a second beating heart: yours.
In quick and steady
counterpoint to my own, its rhythm said,
"I am here. I am strong." I held my breath to hear,
and began to believe
in this new, sweet sound, and to pray it would
never stop.

Today, I kneel
laughing as you wrestle me close with chubby arms.
Suddenly I hear again that joyful pounding, now
measuring a life separate from mine,
each beat saying, "I am safe. I am happy."
And I bless the promise of the time to come,
even as the moment passes
and hurries you away.

Tomorrow, I will stand
and hug you (now the taller one) good-bye.
For as long as you let me, I will listen
trying once more to believe
the proud drumming that says,
"I am ready. Let me go."
Then I will remember
when first I heard that sound, and what I prayed for.
And in the stillness as you go, as if in answer,
I will hear again within me
the echo of a second heart,
beating now in unison with mine:
Strong and steady, joyful and proud,
it is my love for you
never stopping
never stopping
never stopping

Elizabeth Wiegard

Vacant House

The house next door is vacant.
I watch the United Van Lines arrive
to pack up our golden friendship,
    stashing our morning coffee breaks in china barrels,
    rolling up our picnics with the carpets,
    crating our hopes, our fears
    in boxes - big and small.
Now the cartons stacked like skeletons of memory,
I watch them load the truck's dark tomb,
watch them roll away—away.
The house next door is empty.
And so is my heart.

Daryl Rohrbacher

Etching by Jan Myers

Daily Bread

Help.
We mothers can dish it out
but we sure can't take it.
As easy as apple pie,
we fill our hearts
with the warm, sticky fillings
of our everyday lives
then, spread the wealth.
Like jam on fresh-baked bread,
we gloss over imperfections,
fill in the cracks,
sweeten the lives
of those around us.
Nurturing comes easy.
Love is the gentle,
rhythmic outpouring
of our hearts.

How simple to be the jam—
ever-flowing, ever reaching out,
subtly finding our niche
in other people's lives.
How difficult to see
that even a mother's life
is, at times,
confined by four corners:
barren and creviced—
desperately in need
of what is indeed
blessed to give
But just as essential
to receive.

Rosa Turner Knapp

Ink drawing by Sandra Littell

May I Join In?

Symptoms
Language delay or difficulty, abnormality
Flapping hands, avoidance of eye contact
In own world
Inability to make peer relationships, to play
Imaginatively
Obsession with spinning or spinning self
Any future independence a big doubt.

Functioning at 50 percent capacity.

You have the symptoms
Indeed (of autism)
But you have a smile that warms me
to the core of my soul.
And a language
Only I can know.
And a special look
Only I can read.
And a special place etched
In the chasms of my spirit.

No matter what paper and files
Say, or what labels are used to describe
your "differentness"
You are the little boy
I patted in my womb
And that I will always ache to hold.
Even when your whole world may stop,
And you can't get out
And the words won't come,
I want you to know
That if you need me to,
I will hold you and sign "juice" with you
And I will even spin with you
Until our worlds collide together.

Connie Post

For My Toddler

Sometimes I feel soft and warm
like a pillow or a homemade quilt
I wrap my arms around you
and comfort you
You snuggle in
and get comfortable

Sometimes I feel hard and brittle
like an apple tree in the winter
you climb up me
and I am afraid I will break
but I can hold you
and wonder of wonders
Sometimes I even blossom

Cynthia Thomas

Ink drawing by Jennie Harriman

Present Perfect

I am not the best
mother
but you make me feel
like I am
when a tug at my hand
says, "Come, let's pretend . . ."
When the secrets we share
light up the air
with unbridled laughter
I've nothing more
to be after
—not being a "better"
    Mom—
just being there
to lend a palm to the tiny tracings
of a chubby finger
is more than enough
There's no greater love
than your tender acceptance
of a less than perfect me

Rosa Turner Knapp

Grating Parmesan

A winter evening,
sky, the color of cobalt,
the night coming down like the lid on a pot.
On the stove, the ghosts of summer simmer:
tomatoes, garlic, basil, oregano.
Steam from the kettle rises,
wreathes the windows.
You come running when I reach for the grater,
"Help me?" you ask, reversing the pronouns,
part of your mind's disordered scramble.
Together, we hold the rind of the cheese,
scrape our knuckles on the metal teeth.
A fresh pungency enters the room.
You put your fingers in the fallen crumbs:
"Snow," you proudly exclaim, and look at me.
Three years old, nearly mute,
but the master of metaphor.
Most of the time, we speak without words.

Outside, the icy stones in the sky
glitter in their random order.
It's a night so cold, the very air freezes flesh,
a knife in the lungs, wind rushing
over the coil of the planet
straight from Siberia,
a high howl from the wolves of the steppes.
As we grate and grate, the drift rises higher.
When the family gathers together,
puts pasta in their bowls,
ladles on the simmered sauce,
you will bless each one
with a wave of your spoon:
"Snowflakes falling
all around."
You're the weatherman
of the kitchen table.
And, light as feathers,
the Parmesan sprinkles down,
its newly fallen snow
gracing each plate.

Barbara Crooker

46

Pencil drawing by Pauline Lorfano

Ink wash by Carolyn S. Grasso

Up in the Night

She rises
Mother goddess in white gown
Puts baby to breast, to sleep
Slays the three-year-old's monster by
    flashlight
Seeds are laid for future
When they'll turn to her
Tearfilled, scared
Why do they . . .?
Why did he . . .?
Emptiness and Fears unsolved by
Milk and Flashlights
The goddess knows
There will come a time
When, up in the night, there will be
Only
Shared tears

Kati Simons

Mommy Writes

Back bent over the bare
boards of a sleeping house
stealing time, like cookies
from a jar, Mommy writes.

Tawnya Israel

Missing

Today you ran happily away
from me in the kitchen
down the long drive to stand
tiny
in the dirt road
where cars zoom.

I called and searched
then ran
my heart on fire
my eyes burning

I couldn't hold you tight enough then.
You take my breath away.

Marcia Crosbie

Preschool Days

I will wait
for my boy by the curb,
I will not surge forward
when the car bearing him
rounds the corner and slows.
I will not throw out my arms
like sticks, like ropes
to the drowning: he
is not drowning,
he is coming home
after preschool
with his friends, laughing,
teasing, he is not looking
for me, not until
the car stops
and he remembers this world
where I live, where he sojourns
so lightly—
until I have grown enough
to let him go

Wendy McVicker

Graphite drawing by Mary Alice Baumgardner

Acrylic on paper by Jan Myers

In the Clerestory of Leaves

We drive to your special education
    preschool
under an arch of maples, half green, half
    turned to gold,
the dark branches bold as the ribs
of a great cathedral, flying buttresses
that bend the light.
You haven't changed in the last two
    years,
developmentally delayed, mildly retarded,
school a struggle to stay in your seat,
say the beginnings of words,
point to colors and shapes.
While you wrestle with scissors,
daub with paste, I sit in the hallway,
trying to write, turn straw into gold.

When our two hours are spent,
we drive back up the hill toward home,
see the stand of mixed hardwoods
in full conflagration: red-gold, burnt
    orange,
blazing against the cobalt sky.
The architect who made these trees
was sleeping when he made this boy.
And my heart, like the leaves, burns and
    burns.

Barbara Crooker

Lost Innocence

How confident is four.
And, I, with the lines
of thirty years more,
am brought to my knees.

"Why did the man do that?"
He asks after a news clip
I assumed to be
background noise.

Absolute evil is hard
to explain—
the motivation of a hermit
to kill fathers,
the explosion leaving
babies and grandmothers
torn limb from limb,
brothers drowned
at a mother's hand.

Technology?
Hating government?
Low self-esteem?
These replies even I
can not comprehend.

"I do not know,"
I answer.

"But why?" he presses.

His question strips me
of my virgin mothering.
I can not conquer this territory
pushing through
my provincial doorstep.

The evil ones have forced
me to my knees
in my own home.
And here,
I hold my son
and pray.

Betty Ellen Walter

Charcoal drawing by Anne Baumgartner

Watercolor by Pauline Lorfano

A Painting of Love

If I were a painter, I could capture the colors,
shimmering silver blue
blazing sunflower yellow
on a palette of swirling sandy whites.

If I were a painter, I could capture their presence,
sitting on the sand
grandmother and granddaughter
timeless portraits of love.

If I were a painter, I could capture their gestures,
an older arm draped over a younger shoulder,
a little hand pointing to the horizon,
two heads looking straight out to sea.

If I were a painter, I could capture it all,
even the mother staring down the cliff,
secretly sharing their smiles,
quietly following their gaze.

If I were a painter, my hand could paint
for the world,
what my soul has painted
for my heart.

Moryt Milo

Nocturne

To stroke my child's hair
in the night
is a hallowed thing
sometimes I rub a finger
on her smooth peach cheek
over nose
and curve of mouth
breathe the sleeping hush
from her nostrils
watch eyes flutter
in faraway fairylands
and lay my face next to hers
touch my lips to buttery skin
share her fanciful pillow
and remember how it was
to be a five-year-old
slumbering angel
worshiped by a congregation
of one

Diana Rogers

Love's Labor

You rinse, I load.
You clear the table,
I put away the leftovers—
        The rhythm of life
You read Babar when you'd
        prefer the sports page.
I check homework instead
        of the TV Guide.
Choices, teamwork, commitment.
Children's bedtime—the storm
        before the quiet.
Together we work then together we
        play.
These labors of love are the
        foreplay I respond to.

Jana Vick

Pencil drawing by Kathy Strahota

Pencil drawing by Amy Ribordy Reese

A Poem For My Husband

While you work, you give us the most
    cherished of all
treasures
TIME
time . . .
For snuggling and cuddling
two morning-tousled lifeforms
beneath magical tents of sheets
Time . . .
To throw away the shopping plans
because it's ugly outside
and there's always tomorrow
Now we have time . . .
For glitter messes
and chocolate batter kisses
Time . . .
to explore puddles
mountains of books
and the depths of our imagination
Your efforts allow me time . . .
To shape and mold
and rock and hold
THANK YOU

Thank you for adhering to unyielding,
    grinding schedules
so that we can dance to the flow of the
    music each day
Thank you, my husband
for fighting traffic, office politics and
    the sterile
business world
to give us . . .
Time
Together
Your sphere of equations and meetings
opens our world
to a deeper understanding of one
    another

Thank you for staring into a computer
    screen every day
So that I can gaze into
our children's big, hungry eyes all day
    long.
Thank you from all of us.
We know how lucky we are.

Carol Mader

Storage Boxes

Storage boxes on the shelf in my closet
Neatly labeled, MATERNITY
    CLOTHES
Tributes to victory over infertility,
Hope rekindled, dreams recaptured,
    heartache renounced.
Storage boxes on the shelf in my
    daughter's closet
INFANT CLOTHING, MISC. LAYETTE
Tiny treasures, testimonies to motherhood
    embraced,
Dreams realized, joy immeasurable
Storage boxes on the closet floor
CLOTHES 12-24 MONTHS, PLAYPEN
    MISC. BABY THINGS
Sweet memories folded, packaged and
    stacked
Savored days still pass too quickly.
Storage boxes in the basement
CRIB, POTTY CHAIR, CLOTHES 2-3
    TODDLER
Chronicles of growth and achievement,
    beginnings, and endings
Our girl-child blossoms as my youth
    fades.
Storage boxes gathering dust
Guardians of hope, protectors of
    dreams
Captive witnesses to silent prayers—

Please God, let me open them again.

Peggy Towers

First Day of Kindergarten

Tears fall silently
As she fills the new lunchbox
Of her last-born child.

Robert Deluty

Watercolor by Pauline Lorfano

Spring Song for Taran

I didn't clean the house today
I didn't do the laundry

You
Lured me out the door
Into a world exploding
In luscious circles of
Green
Pulsing strong with sap
Dizzy with the turn of the seasons

We rolled in fresh cut grass
Caught pink blossoms in our hair
Stirred some mud puddles . . .
Spun transfixed together
Through one soft sun-touched moment of time
Tasting the sweet green change in the wind

I didn't help you count today
I didn't cut your nails
I swam wild with you
Through a luster of chlorophyll
Played hide and seek
With this swirling
Sweet green poem

And when your face turned up
Smudged with earth
And smelling of spring
And you said
"Hug!"
I was there

Edwina Peterson Cross

Ink drawing by Sandra Littell

Things To Do Today, Tomorrow, And Always

pick up the dry cleaning
go to store:
    apples
    bread
    milk
forgive my husband
    for being a lout when I deserved a saint
    for not noticing I had my hair done
    for forgetting to put the seat down
thank him
    for being a saint when I deserved a lout
    for not noticing I gained five pounds
    for remembering where I left my glasses
dentist appointment at two o'clock
kids to the mall for sneakers
notice:
    how my daughter carefully bites each
        Peanut M&M in half
    and chews the first half thoroughly
    before putting the other half in her
        mouth.
    how tall one son has gotten
        and the way he nods his head in
    agreement
        exactly the way his father does
    how deep the other son's voice has
        become
    and how much less he needs me for
        everyday things
    and how much more for the
        important stuff
mail manuscript by five p.m.
buy stamps
clean the oven
pay attention
    the next time he decides to open up
    the next time she tries to tell me a joke
        she can't remember
    the next time he wants to be told "no"
        but doesn't know it
    the next time he asks for help with
        words
defrost something for dinner
realize
  it's all over too soon.

Cathy Drinkwater Better

The Lost Children

the ones we never speak of – –
miscarried, unborn,
removed by decree,
taken too soon, crossed over.
They slip red mittens in our hands,
smell of warm wet wool,
are always out of sight.
We glimpse them on escalators,
over the shoulders of dark-haired women;
they return to us in dreams.
We hold them, as they evanesce;
we never speak their names.
How many children do you have?
Two, we answer, thinking three,
or three, we answer, thinking four;
they are always with us.
The lost children
come to us
at night
and whisper
in the shells
of our ears.
They are waving goodbye
on schoolbuses,
they are separated from us
in stadiums,
they are lost in shopping malls
with unspeakable pools,
they disappear on beaches,
they shine at night in the stars.

Barbara Crooker

Watercolor by Kelly Gallaher

Watercolor by Joyce Elliott

Retrospective

Oh, my grubby darlings —
I remember when you were a dream.
Now you're sandbox fingernails and hair in the eyes,
untucked shirts and untied shoes.
How did you appear?
In high-school fantasies did I ever believe
you would outgrow shoes
miss the john
tickle my ear with your
wet whispery
unintelligible secrets,
and have sticky fat fingers I'd find curled in mine?
How does a misty scene of faceless children
and vague hopes
become grape-jelly-stained flesh?
What brought you,
with your wheat-stalk cowlicks,
to this midday moment?
Bone of my bone,
flesh of my own flawed flesh,
biology alone does not explain
what paints a highway of peanut butter
from left ear to right
on the cheeks of an idea.

Anita DeLuna Becthold

Boxes

Folding the laundry is the dullest chore
In the world
And yet, as I stand here bored
My hands moving automatically
I smile . . .
When I think how many, many times
These tiny sox have been folded

My sister's hands
Far away from my mountains full of snow
In the green by the sea
And the baby who first wore these little overalls
Is almost six feet tall

I cried when I folded away the tiniest baby dresses
For the last time
Tears on the pink and the lace
But, the emptiness inside was gradually replaced
With a warm, deep glow
for they go now to you
Tiny new pink niece

And soon another sister's hands
Will fold these tiny sox,
These little overalls,
In her rolling green hills

Across the country boxes go
Full of tiny sox,
Little overalls,
Whose material is strong and lasts

Like our love

Edwina Peterson Cross

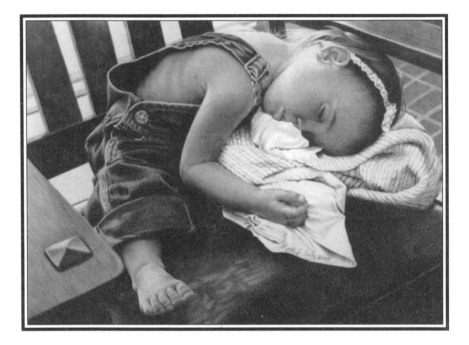

Colored pencil drawing by Lynn Van Couvering   71

Ink drawing by Susan Somerfield Stoffle

there is no party

there is no party for me to plan
isn't that a mother's job
invite the children, serve the cake, play
    the games
sing

where are you
I miss you

Three . . . you would have been three
    today
talking, dancing, learning to sing
taunting your sister and
blowing kisses

where are you
I miss you

my work is not complete
until I can celebrate your birth
with you

but you are missing
I am alone

where is the three year old I would
    hold
where is the little girl I might scold
where is grandma's little angel
where do you travel, Simone

do you know I love you
do you know I miss you
do you know I am trying to make sense
    of your death
do you know you would be three years
    old
and what a wonderful party we could
    have had

do you know each time a child is born,
    I cry
do you know each time a child dies, I
    cry
do you know I miss you

there will not be a party this June
but there will be a mother
missing you with one less thing to do

kiss you

and one more thing to do

miss you

Cristy Pollak

to Simone Donna Pollak
born and died June 29, 1988,
due to Potter's Syndrome

First Camp-Out

She's six
in the dark
in a tent
in a sleeping bag
that might not be warm enough
on ground cold and lumpy
yielding only ants and vermin
what's burrowing beneath her
what's coiling through the brush
rattling in the crackling sun
Did someone hear a coyote's eerie song
see his ears
trotting through trees
700 acres burned here last week
it's tinder dry
brown and craving another
bleached ignition
the mountain lions are coming down
to creeks and homes and pools
driven by tweedy autumn's thirst
will they prowl and purr
and sharpen their teeth
on these little scouts
in their canvas armor
She's six
in the dark
in a tent
and I'm under a comforter
with a trashy midnight talk show
wondering if she's breathing
her deepest sleeping breath
wondering if she's wondering
about me
knowing she'll come back
more independent
closer to seven
ready to purge me of these
maternal nightmares.

Diana Rogers

The Vineyard

Sitting at the kitchen table,
trying to write
in time knifed
from the household loaf;
the dull words cloud in coffee cups.
Images congeal;
the allotted hour sifts away.
Time melts like butter on the stove,
and poetry is sucked down the drain
with the grounds and rinds.

But underneath
poems are sprouting;
their tough seeds sink, composted.
Sprouts glow in the dark
like waxy candles
and bloom, full grown,
without invitation.

Stalks curl through my hands,
pierce my feet,
sink roots in the blood-dry earth.

It is time for fixing supper,
but I can't quit now,
I am bursting with growth; I can't stop,
new lines push out of my fingers,
the tendrils wind out in the breeze,
every inch growing.

Barbara Crooker

Ink drawing by Sandra Littell

Three Mothers

Mother

Fearless.
And I was fearless by your side
if not fearless, then protected.
Still at 30 and 60 the umbilical pulls us
    back together for stolen hours
    alone
Harkening again to our 9 months of
    inseparableness, we make time
    go backwards
    we make time stand still.
More often, now, I hear your words
    when I talk
See your profile in my latest picture
And Relax, knowing well who I will
    become,
fearless.

Mother
in-law

Wisdom
and eyes of faith
    through you I see the Everlasting.
I sit at your table and listen
    to wars and dreams and children.
A gift from my husband you are and
    he
    your first gift to me.
You call me your daughter-in-love
    and love is stronger now
than the law that bound us.

Step
Mother

Grafted in
    with no vested interest,
    no mirrored reflection to draw
you,
You were free to love me
    or not.
Strangers living together,
cautiously we explored the unknown,
    Each other
And finding safety, gentleness, haven,
    we rewrote the fairy tale.

Kelly A. Kim

Ink drawing by Susan Somerfield Stoffle

The Children of The Challenger League Enter Paradise

Here in Little League heaven,
there will be no strikes against you
before you're up at bat,
no standards and regulations
to struggle against, no segregation,
no special education.
All the empty wheelchairs, braces,
    walkers.
No seat belts, head supports, drool
    bibs.
The crooked, straight. The rough
    places, plain.
No toy bats, wobbly tees, whiffle balls,
everybody-scores-outs-don't-count
    rules.
These are the Major Leagues, stadium
    packed,
bases loaded, and the lights are on in
    the firmament.
Samantha winds up to pitch. David hits
a hard line drive deep to center. Adam
throws to Trevor, straight and true.
But here comes Jodie, stealing second,
then third, no longer held aloft by her
    dad,
while her legs windmill in the dust, no,
she's faster than the ink on a new
    contract,
she's sliding into home,
her smile bright enough
to power Detroit.

Barbara Crooker

Watercolor by Carla Jaranson

Ten Years of April

Your flaxen baby curls
Have turned to cascades of gold dust
Falling like silken water down your
    back
Chubby toddler legs
Stretch out to streamline
The blooming dance you begin to
    weave

Should I search your changing face,
Sighing as I see it recast,
Mourning its transformation?
Must I face with fear that new cocoon
That sometimes masks your incan-
    descence?
Shall I weep at the trembling wet
    butterfly
That will soon emerge
Whispering . . .
"Where has my baby gone?"

Once, when you were only mine
I committed my life
As a pledge to your potential
I cradled your quiescent probabilities
Nurtured the grain of your growing
    gifts
Then, your eyes were turned to me
    alone
In undiluted trust

Now, you search
And you scrutinize
You paint
And you ponder
You dance
And you dream
With a growing gift for giving
You aspire to heal each pain filled
    heart
Conquer prejudice
Blot out injustice
You seek to smother hatred
In a sea of sunshine

And I in humble affirmation
Now give back that trust in full
    measure
To your seacrystal eyes

Wings of wonder are unfolding
From the promise that lay dormant
In the infant that I loved
My baby is not gone
My child is
Becoming

No
I will not cry
When the chrysalis cracks
For as you lift to dance the air
All the stars in the sky will sing

Edwina Peterson Cross

Applewood

Out of the bare trees,
pink buds swell,
hold on and on
before they blush,
then blossom out,
unfolding to starry hearts,
transforming the orchard
in ruffles and lace,
lasting three days . . .

And our daughters, too,
unfolding,
too large for swings,
too small for formals,
appling out
their breasts, pippins,
their limbs unpruned . . .

How slowly the apples grow,
taking rain inside,
wrapped in sun.
In August, they look grown,
but a taste puckers the tongue.
Not until storms and frost
will the sugar run.

And these young girls,
sneaking mascara,
sleeping with bunnies,
time is heavy and slow . . .

The apples hang on the boughs;
the weight, the weight,
it stretches the tree.
But these are the branches
that will not break;
this is the cycle
that can't be broken;
these are the apples,
full of juice and spirit,
a harvest of summer
to savor all year . . .

And, we will all,
mothers and daughters,
end like Amish apple dolls,
wrinkled and dried,
but turned into ourselves,
as red winesaps on the bough.

Barbara Crooker

Colored pencil drawing by Connie Cogger

The Umbilical Cord

Oh, Doctor, are you sure . . .
      the day he was born and you cut the cord—
      that cord that connects child to mother—
did you make a clean cut, complete?

Because sometimes I wonder
      when the sound of his cry would cause
      the strange pain, prickly pins,
      "letting down" the milk to meet his need.
      And when, as he advanced to solids and fed with a spoon
      my mouth popped open
      with every attempt to spoon food into his;
      my tongue licked the corners of my mouth
      when the baby food spilled out on his face.

If the cord was cleanly cut, complete
      why the sinking sick stomach in me
      at the sight of *his* blood after a fall?
      Why is my mouth dry
      when he is the one on stage to say the lines?
      Why are my palms sweating
      when he is the pitcher on the mound?
      Why does my heart ache
      when his is broken?

Doctor, could you check?
I think the cord is still intact.

Jana Vick

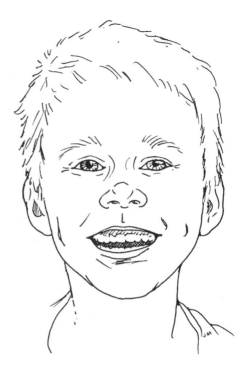

Paradox

Drops of water pool around the sink,
telltale signs that you parted your own hair today.
Comb in hand, squinting at the mirror,
trying to look like the young man
that nature says you are becoming.

But on the floor are tiny paper soldiers,
poised astride their horses for imaginary battle,
waiting only for you to call them out with your bugle cry.

An hour ago, you sprawled face down beside their fort,
a general with troops to command.
Our busyness swirled around you, unheeded.

Now one last look, a final touch,
and out the door.
Your jaunty walk says teenager,
but it's my little boy that wildly waves good-bye.

Kathryn Ahrens

Ink drawing by Jami Moffett

Ink drawing by Laura Ross

For Lezlie at Twelve

I brought you into a world
Of riots and drive by shootings
What made me believe
When I had navigated the labyrinth
Of choking, colic and croup
That I was done with terror?

I send you out each day
Book bag across your back
And cello under your arm
I am seeking for amulets and charms
I am weaving prayers
Through the colorless dawn

    Keep her safe
    Keep her true
    She is so good
    She bruises so easily
    Oh, You who watch for
        sparrows falling
        and number the hairs of heads
    Don't let anyone hurt her

Then I watch you
Lean the golden wood against your body
Pulling rich sweet strands of Mozart from
    the air
Building a breath of timeless beauty
With your own strong hands

Your eyes lift from the pages of your book
Coming back to this world slowly
Bringing with them
Depth beyond your years
And a wisdom you were born with

In the end
Darkness can only be fought with light
And you
Fragile flame
With a core of blazing steel
Glow brighter every day

Leaving my door each morning
Going out into the world
With knowledge slung across your back
Beauty under your arm
Wisdom and laughter
In your eyes

You are your own talisman
Your shining self
The radiant answer
To my prayer

Edwina Peterson Cross

Nearly Thirteen

Needing me,
but not sure
how to show it,
losing him
but not sure if
he knows it . . .
our dance of independence
still plays on.

Gayle Blair Urban

Open Door

Your childhood is leaving quickly
through the cracks
in your voice.
I gather what I can:
snapshots, hairclippings, artwork.
You sleep sprawled out
on the bed that used to swallow you
I sigh a prayer into your dreams,
cover the feet
that will walk out my door
and long,
even now
for their return.

Vicky Vincent

Pencil drawing by Leslie Dugas

Daughter's Dance

Fifteen.
New Year's Eve.
Her eyes, like the cider,
sparkling with possibilities.
Donuts, streamers, music.
Layers of laughter,
kinetic bodies dancing the ageless dance.

Forty-five.
I sit like an exiled Buddha,
visible but nonexistent.
Back aching, listing resolutions.
Nibbling carrots.
Sighing the hours toward midnight.

Once I was fresh-skinned,
twirling through rose gardens fragrant
with the promise of prize-winning blooms.

I don't remember choosing this soft, fat
upholstered chair.
When did I stop dancing?

Patricia Hubbard

Marriage Geometry

We begin. Two points connected by
the straight line of love.
The baby's arrival constructs a triangle.
We are forced to redefine our assumptions.
The second birth completes our geometric
progression. Rectangular now. We are solid,
cumbersome.
These fulfilling, frustrating years bisect our
energy. If the whole is equal to the sum of its
parts, then each personality must be accommodated.
We parent through each logical step.
The first born leaves to become his own
whole number.
We three remainders realign angles,
forming a tentative diagram.
Soon, the second child breaks free.
Time to check our work. Did the theorem
of commitment prove valid?
We conclude. Two points connected
by the straight line of love.

Patricia Hubbard

Ink drawing by Sandra Littell

As we gather in
our mothers' kitchens

fill a cellar
with roots and wine
bring in sunwarm stones
to place around my hearth
I want a reservoir of earth
beneath my fingernails for
when the winter comes

when days grow short
not just with busyness
of schools and shoes preserves
and bulbs but with lengthening shadows
when hands are busy making ready and
all the day is filled with filling
mouths and jars and cookies and
the ice cream man twinkles off
to warmer climes doesn't
he know how frail my
shelter is?

twigs snap
leaves and fires crackle
hear the apple bites

the closet grows
pickles green and briny
the basement harbors dandelion wine
the tubers are cautioned not to trouble
themselves with roots; I kiss each eye
my bulbs live self-contained as fatty bears
and it is here that you will know me.

Sauci Churchill

Colored pencil drawing by Connie Cogger

Commencement

She opened doors for us,
this child, our firstborn,
in forging three from two.
With crayons thick and bright,
this silken-haired daughter
colored our pathway into her world.
Tugging at our sleeves, she led us
to the wisdom of the Creator:
the tulip and the buttercup,
the turtle and the worm.
As she grew, we grew,
measure for measure,
each milestone securing
the mystery that is family.
In time, she even unlatched our own past
and embroidered it to her
in kaleidoscope colors,
the golden strands of music and laughter
outshining life's dark thread of pain.

She opens doors for us,
this child, our firstborn,
and leads us in the next hesitant step:
letting go.
The door stands ajar.

Gail Parker

Ink drawing by Susan Somerfield Stoffle

My Oldest Child

My oldest child has rented an apartment.
We helped him move and took him out to
    eat.
And as we parted ways, I knew in coming
    days,
His room would be my cozy new retreat.

Of course I'll need new wallpaper and
    curtains.
My desk will fit quite nicely near the door.
And later, if I like, a stationary bike
And Oriental carpet for the floor.

But as I look around his room and ponder,
I see a toddler busily at play.
I daydream for awhile, and I begin to smile.
I won't be changing anything today.

Linda Sultan

On Giving Birth to Grandparents

If you wait
as I did
I'll be sixty when my
grandchildren are born
The day I realized that
I signed up
for an exercise class
The power of a generation of children
yet unborn, twice removed, calling
me to rise early
each day and prepare
my arms to hold them
my legs to run with them.

Don't laugh
because my children are
one and four and I
am already counting my grandchildren.
My mother created her
grand-
children
while she created me
My own are
here
eggs nestled
in my daughter's womb.

My son runs
to my parents screaming
Gramma Grampa
To the parents who gave me
life
I have given family
inexpressible gift of
a safe harbor when
the world is hard.

In the circle
of my husband's family
myself, in-law
my children, in.
How did they forge from
bonds of water
bonds of blood?

Oh, what a sparkling
web we weave when first
we set out to
conceive.

Robin Alpern

Ink drawing by Pam Collar

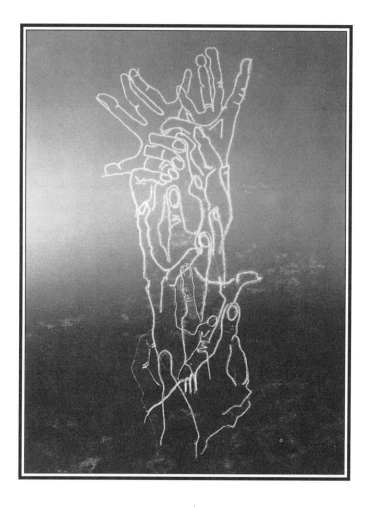

Monotype by Jan Myers

Mothers

See how we build

Ours are not the rewards
Of dollars or praise
A baby's sated milk deep sigh
A toddler's sticky kisses
Fleeting moments like butterflies' wings
That touch between our fingers
Brush bright against our lips
And then are gone
Into the sunmist of time

The ribbons of our teaching
They will gather and weave into themselves
To be claimed as their own
In the end
The production of our lives
Will stand alone
And we will silently sit the shadows

For it is the nature of things
That open hands
at last
are empty

And yet
We work on
In some strange way fulfilled
From the glittering pain of beginning
Towards a harvest we will never see
Vital links
In the mystery chain
Of creation

Artisans of solid dreams
Oh See!
See how we build

Edwina Peterson Cross

Index

About Mothers At Home

Founded in 1984 as a national nonprofit 501 C(3) organization, Mothers At Home is committed to:

- affirming the choice to be home throughout the many stages of motherhood;
- providing mother-to-mother support, education, and networking;
- correcting society's misconceptions and refuting stereotypes about at-home mothers;
- serving as advocates for children concerning their needs for generous amounts of their parents' time; and
- encouraging and enabling mothers to preserve and improve the opportunity for all women to choose home.

Mothers At Home accomplishes these goals through its publishing efforts as well as by speaking out to mothers' groups, the media, public policy organizations, government officials, and others.

Other Publications

Welcome Home, our award-winning journal, brings affirmation each month in its beautifully-illustrated, advertisement-free pages. Readers tell us how WH gives them emotional support and a feeling of community with other mothers, provides practical information and role models, and empowers them to speak out on behalf of their families and themselves. In WH, mothers share essays about their struggles and successes, problem-solving, humor, and poetry, as well as informative articles about family life, media and public policy issues. Written, edited and illustrated by mothers, Welcome Home is the professional journal for the woman who has chosen to devote her time and talents to nurturing her family.

What's A Smart Woman Like You Doing At Home? was written by the founders of Mothers At Home in 1986 after they had been surprised and inspired by the thousands of mothers who contacted them. In this book, the authors dispel the stereotypes about at-home mothers and uncover the truth behind the misuse of statistics in the ongoing debate about women and their work/home choices. The authors give plenty of evidence to support their contention that nurturing children requires much more time, intelligence, and skill than this generation of mothers was led to believe. Their honest look at women's lives demonstrates how staying home can offer many opportunities for widening personal and professional horizons.

Discovering Motherhood was created by the staff of Mothers At Home especially for women in their first years of motherhood. They realized that new mothers, faced with significant physical, emotional, and social changes, are especially in need of assistance while they make the transition into motherhood. Discovering Motherhood explores the realities and rewards of a home-centered life. Lovely drawings illustrate the personal narratives, essays, informative articles, humor and poetry from more than forty authors.

Reprints from *Welcome Home* cover popular topics, with articles chosen from over a decade of back issues. These reprints are carefully edited and many provide up-to-date resource lists. Request a current list of reprints by mail or by calling our 800 number.

Speaking Out for Mothers

Mothers At Home is a strong and effective voice in both public policy discussions and media representation. MAH works to:

- Challenge the "typical" housewife and "typical" working mother stereotypes, as well as the misuse of statistics regarding the care of children.
- Research the needs and attitudes of at-home mothers through detailed surveys and send this information to policy makers and the media.
- Educate the media and others about the subtle, complex, and rewarding work of nurturing children.
- Present information and analyses to our readers through the pages of WH as well as to the media in editorials and letters to the editor.

A Family-Friendly Organization

The Mothers At Home volunteers and staff have work options which include part-time and job-share positions, flexible schedules, flex-time and home-based work. The organization is housed in a family-friendly office with a large, sunny playroom in view of meeting and work rooms.

Contact Mothers At Home

You may write to Mothers At Home at:

> Mothers At Home
> P.O. Box 2192
> 8310A Old Courthouse Road
> Vienna, VA 22182

or call our order/information line: **800-783-4666**